# Consonant and Digraphs

## Written by Dona Herweck Rice

**Teacher Created Materials, Inc.**
6421 Industry Way
Westminster, CA 92683
www.teachercreated.com
©1997 Teacher Created Materials, Inc.
Reprinted, 2000
Made in U.S.A.
**ISBN 1-57690-242-0**

*Illustrator:*
*Sue Fullam*

*Cover Artist:*
*Chris Macabitas*

*Editor:*
*Karen Goldfluss, M.S. Ed.*

*Imaging:*
*Ralph Olmedo, Jr.*

**Note to Parents and Teachers:**

The books in this series were designed to help parents and teachers reinforce basic skills for their children and students. *Consonant Blends and Digraphs* reviews beginning and end blends and digraphs. The exercises in this book can be done sequentially or can be taken out of order, as needed. In order to complete all exercises, children will need a pencil, crayons, scissors, and glue.

The letter and word cards on the inside covers of this book are included for review. Cut them apart and use them for matching activities. Children can also match each word to the pictures on pages 25 and 27, or they can match the letters to objects around the house or school. They can draw and color additional pictures, as desired.

Here are some useful ideas for making the most of the books in this series.

- Help beginning readers with the instructions.

- Review the work the child has done. Whenever possible, work with the child.

- Allow the child to use whatever writing instruments he or she prefers. For example, colored pencils can add variety and pleasure to drill work.

- Pay attention to the areas in which the child has the most difficulty. Provide extra guidance and exercises in those areas.

Color the pictures that begin with the **bl** and **br** sounds.

# Color the pictures that begin with the **cl** and **cr** sounds.

Color the pictures that begin with the **dr** and **tr** sounds.

# Color the pictures that begin with the **fl** and **fr** sounds.

 Color the pictures that begin with the
**gl** and **gr** sounds.

Color the pictures that begin with the **pl** and **pr** sounds.

Color the pictures that begin with the **sk**, **sl**, and **st** sounds.

Color the pictures that begin with the **sm** and **sn** sounds.

Color the pictures that begin with the **sp** and **sw** sounds.

Say the name of the picture.

Circle the **beginning** sound.

| | | |
|---|---|---|
| bl    br | cl    cr | dr    tr |
| fl    fr | gl    gr | pl    pr |
| sk    sl | sm    sn | sp    st |

Say the name of the picture.

Circle the **beginning** sound.

| | | |
|---|---|---|
| fl    fr | sm    sn | dr    tr |
| sk    sl | bl    br | gl    gr |
| pl    pr | cl    cr | sp    sw |

Say the name of the picture.

Circle the **beginning** sound.

| dr | tr | fl | fr | sk | sl |

| cl | cr | sp | sw | gl | gr |

| pl | pr | sm | sn | bl | br |

Draw a line between the pictures with the same **beginning** sounds.

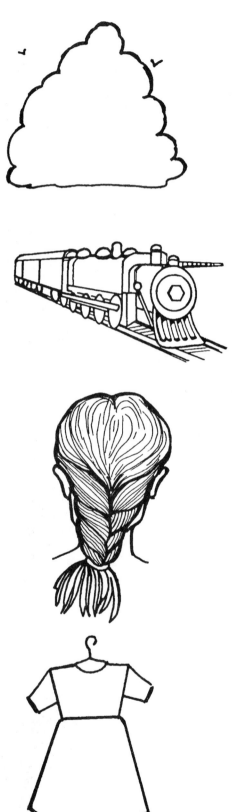

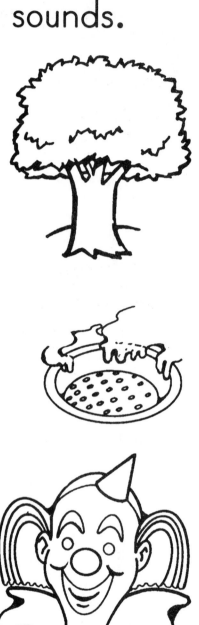

 Draw a line between the pictures
with the same **beginning** sounds.

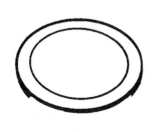

Say the name of the picture.

Write the **beginning** sounds.

| | | |
|---|---|---|
| _____ow | _____ate | _____ose |
| _____og | _____ow | _____ink |
| _____op | _____ock | _____oon |

Say the name of the picture.

Write the **beginning** sounds.

| | | |
|---|---|---|
| _____ unk | _____ an | _____ ed |
| _____ ame | _____ aid | _____ ib |
| _____ ayon | _____ ate | _____ oke |

Say the name of the picture.

Write the **beginning** sounds.

| | | |
|---|---|---|
| _____oke | _____ing | _____ain |
| _____ame | _____y | _____ake |
| _____ain | _____ill | _____own |

Color the pictures that begin with the **sh** and **ch** sounds.

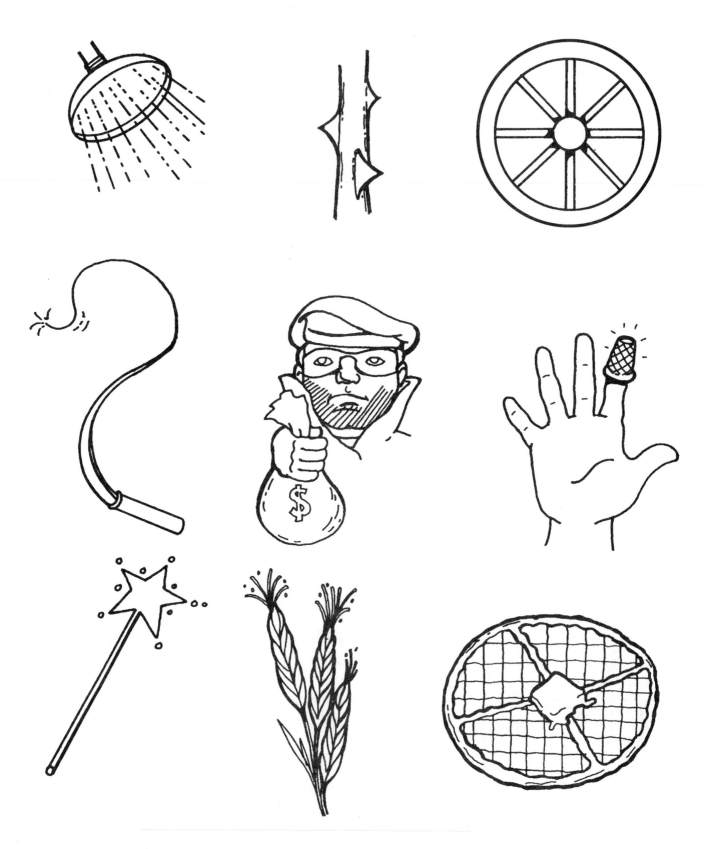

Color the pictures that begin with the **th** and **wh** sounds.

Say the name of the picture.

Circle the **beginning** sound.

| | | |
|---|---|---|
| ch     sh | wh     sh | ch     th |
| th     sh | ch     wh | th     sh |
| ch     sh | sh     th | wh     th |

Say the name of the picture.

Circle the **ending** sound.

| ch | sh | ch | sh | ch | th |
|----|----|----|----|----|----|
| th | sh | ch | sh | th | sh |
| ch | sh | sh | th | ch | th |

Say the name of the picture.

Write the **beginning** sounds.

| | | |
|---|---|---|
| _____ark | _____ild | _____orn |
| _____eep | _____in | _____ick |
| _____ip | _____oe | _____one |

Say the name of the picture.

Write the **ending** sounds.

| | | |
|---|---|---|
| ba_____ | mo_____ | di_____ |
| fi_____ | mat_____ | chur_____ |
| ca_____ | clo_____ | lat_____ |

# Color and cut out. Match to the cards on the covers.

26

# Color and cut out. Match to the cards on the covers.

28

Color the pictures that **begin** with the same sounds to make three in a row.

Color the pictures that **begin** with the same sounds to make three in a row.

# Color the pictures that **end** with the same sounds to make three in a row.

Color the pictures that **end** with the same sounds to make three in a row.